Merseyside Electrics

Jonathan Cadwallader and Martin Jenkins

Ian Allan PUBLISHING

Front cover: The present network of suburban electric lines serving Merseyside developed over many decades. The area has a long, proud and fascinating history with several significant "firsts". The under-river tunnel linking Birkenhead to Liverpool opened in 1886, Faced by financial ruin owing to the choking atmosphere in the smoke-filled tunnel, the Mersey Railway became the first company in Britain to convert entirely from steam to electric traction. Representatives of the original American-style electric rolling stock survived in service until 1957. In May 1955, a train of vintage Edwardian carriages rolled into Birkenhead North. *Ray DeGroote, Online Transport Archive*

Back cover: Although it closed in 1956, The Liverpool Overhead Railway remains a firm favourite. This view of the world's first electrically-powered elevated railway was taken at the north end in July 1956. This was where the Overhead ran from Seaforth Sands to Seaforth and Litherland over tracks owned and electrified by the Lancashire and Yorkshire Railway. The L&Y North Mersey Branch seen on the right was electrified over much of its length and sustained several passenger services. Rimrose Road Junction signal box seen in the background controlled connections between the branch and the LOR whilst the embankment stretching away into the distance took the branch over the Liverpool-Southport electrified line which still operates today. The last electric activity at this location came to end with closure of the LOR on 30 December 1956. *J. B. C. McCann*

Previous page: Restored to LMS livery, preserved 1939 stock Driving Trailer 29896 leads Driving Motor 28361 past RAF Woodvale, just north of Freshfield, on a special service to Formby in July 1986. Up until the 1970s there were gaps in the conductor rails in line with the end of the RAF station's runway in case a plane overshot and landed upon the track. Emergency stop signals for trains could be operated from the airfield's control tower. The two cars were originally preserved by the National Railway Museum and after several years of open storage are currently in poor condition, but the Friends of the 502 Group have now secured them for restoration. *Rob Marsh*

First published 2010

ISBN 978 0 7110 3417 4

© Ian Allan Publishing Ltd 2010

Published by Ian Allan Publishing

an imprint of Ian Allan Publishing Ltd, Hersham, Surrey KT12 4RG.
Printed in England by Ian Allan Printing Ltd, Hersham, Surrey KT12 4RG.

Visit the Ian Allan Publishing website at www.ianallanpublishing.com

Distributed in the United States of America and Canada by BookMasters Distribution Services.

ACKNOWLEDGEMENTS

The authors wish to thank all those who have loaned slides for reproduction, especially Ray DeGroote, whose precious images made several trips across the Atlantic so that most of a colour cast could be removed digitally. Thanks are also due also to Andy and Mair McCann for loan of slides taken by John McCann and to the Parker family for access to the Ted Baxendale collection. They are indebted to Michael Eyre for his image restoration work on many of the older slides.

Some slides are reproduced courtesy of Colour-Rail and Online Transport Archive (OTA) of which one of the authors is a Trustee. Both authors have donated their fees for this book to OTA. Information about the Archive, which was established in 2000 to ensure that transport collections of slides, negatives and cine films are secured for posterity, can be obtained from The Secretary, 8 Aughton Court, Church Road, Upton, Wirral CH49 6JY.The authors are grateful to Chris Poole for the cartography. They also wish to thank those who have provided invaluable information for the captions: Bill Barlow, Aussie Billington, John Forrester, Tony Gahan, Alan Hodges, Rob Marsh, Bruce Maund, Glynn Parry and John Ryan. Special thanks are due to Bill Cadwallader and Charles Roberts.

BIBLIOGRAPHY

In compiling this book the authors have drawn upon several publications, including the outstanding quintet of books by John W. Gahan – *Seaport to Seaside, The Line Beneath the Liners, Seventeen Stations to Dingle, Rails to Port and Starboard, Steel Wheels to Deeside* (published by Countyvise between 1982 and 1992); *An Illustrated History of Liverpool's Railways* by Paul Anderson (Irwell Press, 1996); *Merseyrail Electrics-The Inside Story* by T.B. Maund (NBC Books, 2001); *Mersey Railway Electric Stock* by JE Cull and B.J. Prigmore (Eltrac, 1968); *The Electric Lines of the Lancashire and Yorkshire Railway* by N.N. Forbes, B.J. Felton, R.W. Rush (Electric Railway Society, 1976); *150 Years of the Lancashire & Yorkshire Railway* by Noel Coates (Hawkshill Publishing, 1997); *The Liverpool Overhead Railway* by C.E. Box (Ian Allan, 1984); *The Mersey Railway* by G.W. Parkin (Oakwood Press, 1966); *Merseyside, The Indian Summer Volumes 1 & 2* by Cedric Greenwood (Silver Link, 2007); *Merseyside's Industrial Past* (Merseyside Industrial Heritage Society, 2007); *The Wirral Railway* by Campbell Highet (Oakwood Press, 1961); *Merseyside & District Railway Stations* by Paul Bolger (The Bluecoat Press, 1994).

Introduction

This book is dedicated to Ray DeGroote, the distinguished American transport photographer and also to the memory of Marie Cadwallader and Jacqueline Jenkins.

Historically, Merseyside played a significant role in the development of electric railways. It was home to the world's first electrically-operated elevated railway; the first railway contract completed by the British Westinghouse Company; the first steam to electric conversion in the UK; the first full-scale operation of the multiple-unit (MU) system; the first conversion from steam to electric of a suburban main line; the first application of automatic signalling and Liverpool Central Low Level was almost certainly the first station in the world where movements were controlled without signalmen. The Lancashire and Yorkshire Railway trains which utilised the Liverpool Overhead Railway structure and the L&Y Aintree-Gladstone Dock service were among the first electric services to be discontinued in the UK.

LIVERPOOL OVERHEAD RAILWAY

Powered at 500V DC, the world's first electrically-operated elevated railway opened in 1893. This standard gauge line with its American-style trains was subsequently extended three times so that by 1905 it ran from Dingle in the south to Seaforth and Litherland in the north. When lightweight L&Y cars began operating over the LOR structure in 1905, the original centre rail, with return through the wheels, was replaced by an outside third rail. Riding some 16ft above the congested roads below, the line offered a swift journey for those employed in the city centre and along the waterfront. The 7 mile line also provided visitors with "unrivalled views of the docks and ships". During the dark days of World War 2, the structure was often damaged but being vital to the war effort, it was rapidly repaired. Changes in the shipping industry as well as working practices in the dock estate led to a post-war decline in passenger numbers, but the line remained profitable. Although post-war plans to purchase new stock proved prohibitive, the Company opted instead to refurbish some of its existing fleet. The LOR was not nationalised in 1948 and the financial burden of replacing much of the decaying structure finally led to the demise of "The Dockers' Umbrella", which ran for the final time on 30 December 1956.

THE MERSEY RAILWAY

Demand for improved cross-river connections led to the opening of the first section of the steam-operated Mersey Railway in 1886. The under-river tunnel with its fierce gradients linked Green Lane, Birkenhead to James Street, Liverpool. By the time the 4½ mile network was completed in 1892, the MR was already in financial difficulties. The public clearly preferred the longer journey by ferry to the choking atmosphere of the smoke-filled tunnel. In 1903, the MR became the first railway in the UK to convert entirely from steam to electric traction and to operate trains in multiple unit formation. The contract was the first to be completed by the British Westinghouse Company which electrified at 650V DC employing the 4-rail system. Starting in 1921, automatic colour light signalling was introduced together with electro-pneumatic points and trainstops; another first saw automated reversals at Liverpool Central Low Level in 1923. The original American-style rolling stock was supplemented over the years with small orders to more modern designs.

THE MERSEY RAILWAY AND THE LMS (WIRRAL DIVISION)

In preparation for electrification on the third rail system of the former Wirral Railway lines to New Brighton and West Kirby and the introduction of new rolling stock by its successor, the London Midland & Scottish Railway, modifications were made to the MR 4-rail system so that the trains from both companies could inter-work over the enlarged electric network. From March 1938, MR trains based at Birkenhead Central operated the Rock Ferry and New Brighton services, whilst LMS built electric sets based at new premises at Birkenhead North operated to West Kirby, except on Sundays when the pattern was reversed. Although the system suffered some serious damage during the war, the under-river section never stopped running. When the Mersey Railway was nationalised in 1948 it became part of the London Midland Region of British Railways. Starting in 1956, the veteran MR stock was replaced by new BR sets very similar to the earlier LMS units of 1938. For some time after nationalisation, MR and LMS traditions and practices survived.

THE LANCASHIRE & YORKSHIRE RAILWAY

The L&Y was at the forefront of main line electrification schemes in Britain. In October 1902 the Company agreed to electrify its busy 18½ mile route from Liverpool Exchange to Southport. Despite having four tracks for several miles, by the beginning of the 20th Century the mix of locals, semi-fasts and expresses were struggling to cope with the volume of traffic. No doubt influenced by the success of the LOR and the recent decision to electrify the MR, a plan was approved to electrify the line at 630V DC and contracts were awarded to Dick, Kerr of Preston. Three months later, a

3½ mile extension from Southport to Crossens was authorised. Progress was rapid and electric services commenced in 1904.

As part of a wider local electrification programme, the L&Y opened a link to the Overhead Railway in 1905. This enabled the LOR service to be extended from Seaforth Sands to Seaforth and Litherland. L&Y trains were able to operate along the LOR to Dingle, firstly from Southport and later, Aintree. The third rail arrived at Aintree in 1906, firstly from Marsh Lane and secondly by the direct route from Sandhills via Walton Junction. Further work saw the remaining sides of the triangle at Meols Cop electrified, whilst the market town of Ormskirk saw its first electric train in 1913. When another short section of the North Mersey Goods line was energised in 1914, a workers-only service operated from Aintree to a new station at Gladstone Dock. This proved to be an early casualty, being withdrawn in 1924, although the L&Y services through to Dingle had been terminated some years earlier. The Liverpool Exchange to Aintree via Marsh Lane service lasted until 1951. However, until 1956, the third rail was retained from Rimrose Road Junction to Aintree so that for one day a year, LOR "Race Day Specials" could transport punters to Grand National meetings. The 1963 Beeching Report into the future of the Railways listed the Exchange-Southport line for closure but wiser counsels prevailed. However, the Southport-Crossens local service was axed when all passenger services on the Southport-Preston line were withdrawn in 1964. During this same period, consideration was also given to de-energising the line to Ormskirk. From the 1950s onwards, increased use of buses coupled with a rise in car ownership led to a decline in usage of the two electric lines.

MERSEYSIDE PASSENGER TRANSPORT AUTHORITY– THE LOOP AND LINK

In 1969, local rail services received a major boost with the creation of the Merseyside Passenger Transport Authority which adopted a bold, imaginative plan for an inter-connected network based upon the construction of The Loop and Link lines under Liverpool city centre. Under the auspices of the PTA, several new stations were built and an Integrated Electronic Control Centre was opened in 1994 at Sandhills to house electrical control and signalling functions. The PTA became the Merseyside Integrated Transport Authority in February 2009.

NORTHERN LINE

As shown on the accompanying map, the lines terminating at Exchange Station were re-routed in 1977 via the Link, a new section of tunnel which served the commercial heart of the city. The Link started north of Exchange and eventually connected into the former MR tunnel serving Central Low Level. Electrified at the same time was the section from Walton Junction to Kirkby. Another length of new tunnel which connected Liverpool Central (the old Low Level) with the former CLC line from Liverpool Central High Level enabled electric services to be extended to Garston in 1978 and Hunts Cross in 1983.

WIRRAL LINE

In 1977, the Wirral services were re-routed round the Loop, a unidirectional, single track tunnel which started and ended at James Street and included interchange facilities at two new stations - Moorfields and Lime Street. The third rail was extended south from Rock Ferry, firstly to Hooton in 1986 and subsequently to Chester in 1993 and Ellesmere Port in 1994.

CITY LINE

As part of a programme to electrify the busy West Coast Main Line on the 25kV AC overhead wire system, in 1962 the former London and North Western Railway line from Liverpool Lime Street to Crewe was energised. In 1966, electric services from Lime Street included expresses to London Euston and Birmingham New Street and stopping trains to Crewe. There was also some loco-hauled freight operation. Local services out of Lime Street, including that to Crewe, were later marketed as part of the City Line. As a result of the failure to electrify other routes out of Liverpool, together with the lack of a nationwide electrification programme, many other Merseyside services remain diesel operated. However, in July 2009 plans were announced to extend the overhead wires east to Manchester via the Liverpool and Manchester Railway route.

This photographic excursion around the electric lines of Merseyside features colour images taken between 1951 and 1994. The journey starts on board the LOR. It then follows those lines on the Liverpool side before venturing "over the water" onto the Wirral Peninsula. The photographs have been chosen to reflect the wide range of locations in different weather conditions as well as the variety of rolling stock, of which some types enjoyed a high degree of longevity, making them firm favourites with enthusiasts and the public.

Jonathan Cadwallader
Great Crosby, Merseyside

Martin Jenkins
Walton-on-Thames, Surrey

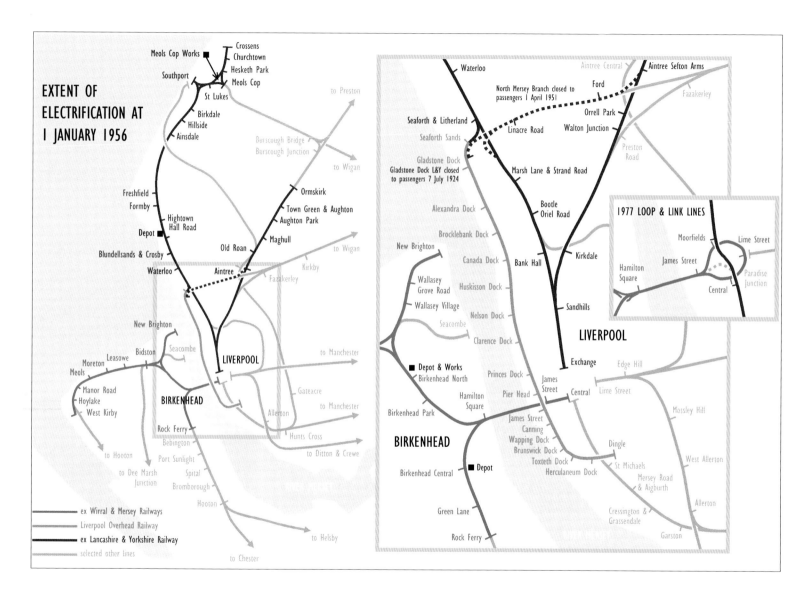

EXTENT OF ELECTRIFICATION AT 1 JANUARY 1956

Meols Cop Works
Crossens
Churchtown
Hesketh Park
Southport
Meols Cop
St Lukes
Birkdale
Hillside
Ainsdale
to Preston
Burscough Bridge
Burscough Junction
to Wigan
Freshfield
Formby
Ormskirk
Town Green & Aughton
Aughton Park
Hightown
Hall Road
Depot
Maghull
Blundellsands & Crosby
Old Roan
Waterloo
Aintree
to Wigan
Kirkby
Fazakerley

New Brighton
Bidston
Seacombe
Leasowe
Moreton
Meols
LIVERPOOL
to Manchester
Manor Road
Hoylake
West Kirby
BIRKENHEAD
Gateacre
Allerton
to Manchester
Rock Ferry
Hunts Cross
Bebington
Port Sunlight
to Hooton
Spital
Bromborough
to Dee Marsh Junction
Hooton
to Ditton & Crewe

ex Wirral & Mersey Railways
Liverpool Overhead Railway
ex Lancashire & Yorkshire Railway
selected other lines

to Helsby
to Chester

Waterloo
Aintree Central
Aintree Sefton Arms
North Mersey Branch closed to passengers 1 April 1951
Ford
Fazakerley
Seaforth & Litherland
Orrell Park
Seaforth Sands
Linacre Road
Walton Junction
Preston Road
Gladstone Dock
Gladstone Dock L&Y closed to passengers 7 July 1924
Marsh Lane & Strand Road
Alexandra Dock
Bootle
Oriel Road
Brocklebank Dock
New Brighton
Canada Dock
Bank Hall
Kirkdale
Wallasey Grove Road
Huskisson Dock
Wallasey Village
Nelson Dock
Sandhills
Seacombe
Clarence Dock
LIVERPOOL
Exchange
Edge Hill
Depot & Works
Birkenhead North
Princes Dock
James Street
Central
Lime Street
Hamilton Square
Pier Head
Mossley Hill
Birkenhead Park
James Street
Canning
Wapping Dock
Dingle
West Allerton
BIRKENHEAD
Brunswick Dock
Toxteth Dock
St Michaels
Depot
Herculaneum Dock
Birkenhead Central
Mersey Road & Aigburth
Allerton
Green Lane
Cressington & Grassendale
Garston
Rock Ferry

1977 LOOP & LINK LINES

Moorfields
Lime Street
Hamilton Square
James Street
Paradise Junction
Central

5

The Liverpool Overhead Railway was the first electrically-powered elevated line in the world. The first section, opened in 1893, was built to carry workers above the congested dock road. The rolling stock was American in style. 46 motor cars were built by Brown Marshall between 1891 and 1895 and various trailers between 1895 and 1936, some later being altered and others modernised. 27 was one of ten motor cars that were widened to take more seating. This view was taken at the south end near Toxteth Station. Latterly, the suffix "Dock" was omitted from station names, so one could travel to Canada or reflect on local and national heroes such as Nelson, Wellington, Canning and Huskisson. Behind the train was the tall Coburg grain silo and the Cheshire Lines Committee Brunswick Dock Goods Station, both since demolished. Electric traction returned to this area when the Northern Line was extended to Garston in 1978 over the former CLC tracks on the right.
Ray DeGroote, Online Transport Archive

Between 1947 and 1955, eight 3-car sets received new Company built "streamlined" bodies with aluminium alloy panels, improved internal fittings including seating and electro-pneumatic sliding doors. 18-5-29 entered service in 1953 although 29 had been rebuilt in 1945. Latterly, these sets comprised a trailer between two motor cars. This section of structure, s-outh of the Pier Head near Wapping Dock station, was severely damaged in 1941 at a time when the LOR carried some 14 million passengers a year. Stations such as James Street and Prince's Dock were destroyed, the latter never reopening. As the docks declined, passenger numbers dropped, although the line still had 25,000 daily passengers during its final year. Faced by a massive bill for renewing its decaying structure, the Company opted for closure. Interestingly, the line was not nationalised in 1948, having been left off "the list" by civil servants in London. *Ray DeGroote, Online Transport Archive*

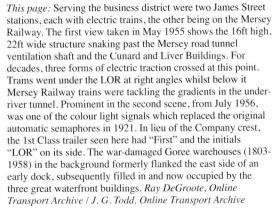

This page: Serving the business district were two James Street stations, each with electric trains, the other being on the Mersey Railway. The first view taken in May 1955 shows the 16ft high, 22ft wide structure snaking past the Mersey road tunnel ventilation shaft and the Cunard and Liver Buildings. For decades, three forms of electric traction crossed at this point. Trams went under the LOR at right angles whilst below it Mersey Railway trains were tackling the gradients in the under-river tunnel. Prominent in the second scene, from July 1956, was one of the colour light signals which replaced the original automatic semaphores in 1921. In lieu of the Company crest, the 1st Class trailer seen here had "First" and the initials "LOR" on its side. The war-damaged Goree warehouses (1803-1958) in the background formerly flanked the east side of an early dock, subsequently filled in and now occupied by the three great waterfront buildings. *Ray DeGroote, Online Transport Archive / J. G. Todd, Online Transport Archive*

Located at the foot of Water Street, Pier Head station was the busiest and most substantial station on the line. Pier Head and Seaforth Sands were the only two stations to have their booking offices on the street as opposed to being at platform level. Advertising posters extolling the line's unique features adorned the staircases on both sides of the wooden structure. With typical Scouse humour, the windswept area underneath, which offered limited protection from the elements, was known as "The Dockers' Umbrella". Liverpool's 18th century Town Hall stands at the top of Water Street. Passing under the bridge with its advert for a local sweet manufacturer was one of Liverpool's streamlined trams. The city's once progressive 97 mile system was replaced by buses between 1948 and 1957. Trams last passed under this bridge in November 1956, a month before the LOR closed on 30 December 1956.
Prince Marshall

9

Significant engineering features encountered on the 30min journey included Dingle tunnel, several lifting bridges, bow-string bridges, a combined lift and swing bridge at Stanley Dock and this "switchback" where the Overhead went under a high level branch serving Bramley-Moore Dock. In May 1955, southbound train 2-1-9 had just crested the incline. When withdrawn the following year, the original unrebuilt motor cars still had wooden seats but more powerful 75 hp motors. Located nearby had been the line's coal-fired generating station which closed in 1927, after which power was obtained from Liverpool Corporation. The LOR was electrified at 500V DC, the current originally being supplied by a centre rail with return through the wheels. When the specially built lightweight Lancashire and Yorkshire Railway trains started operating over the line in 1905, they drew power from an outside live rail and the LOR followed suit. The centre rail, retained for earthing purposes, lasted until resignalling in 1921. *Ray DeGroote, Online Transport Archive*

This north end view taken in 1951 shows 25-10-27 perched imperiously above a trio of Mersey Docks & Harbour Board 0-6-0 saddle tanks. Smoke from locomotives working under the structure, combined with salt from the river, contributed to its corrosion. One of the authors (MJ) remembers riding on the LOR. "Glued to the window on the west side, dockside activity flashed past including all manner of ships, bustling tugs, *Mammoth* the giant floating crane, Clarence Dock Power Station belching smoke, lift and swing bridges and every type of warehouse and transit shed.

Sometimes, little steam locomotives were glimpsed hard at work and during foggy weather, sonorous blasts from hooters and whistles shattered the muffled silence. On the east side were more warehouses, dock-related workshops, mills and factories, pubs, cafes and houses of ill-repute. Below, the dock road appeared clogged with a mix of lorries, steam waggons and horse-drawn carts, and queues formed as trains trundled slowly into goods yards. For all our visitors a ride on the Overhead was a must." *G. Hunt, Colour-Rail IR755*

The carriage shed and workshops at Seaforth Sands were built in 1926 on the site of the original station. This view, taken on 14 May 1955, shows three motor cars of which the middle one, No 3, is preserved. The track was unballasted and laid on wooden sleepers fixed to the decking. On the right can be seen the later Seaforth Sands station, built when LOR trains were extended to the L&Y's Seaforth and Litherland Station in 1905. The signal box controlled reversals at the station as well as shed movements. Today, the former Seaforth transport hub has gone, the area now being within the secure part of the current dock estate. Formerly, thousands used the LOR as well as Corporation trams and buses. Between 1900 and 1925, the LOR had its own feeder tram service to Waterloo and Great Crosby with a depot just to the north of the original station. *Ray DeGroote, Online Transport Archive*

Two views of Seaforth and Litherland which, at this time, had an island as well as two outer platforms. In the first, taken in May 1955, all lines still carried a third rail with Liverpool-Southport trains using those on the left and LOR trains those on the right to Seaforth Sands. The tracks on the bridge in the background were energised and once carried L&Y services from Aintree to Gladstone Dock and Dingle and until 1956, the annual LOR Grand National specials to Aintree. Until 1951, EMUs on a Liverpool-Aintree via Marsh Lane service had also diverged from the Southport line just beyond the bridge. In 2010, the Southport line remains but the de-electrified Marsh Lane to Aintree section is mothballed and the signal box and semaphores vanished long ago. The second view, taken in late 1956, shows the site of the outer platform destroyed during the Blitz and never rebuilt. Set 18-5-29 was at the Overhead terminus on the west side of the island platform. Today, trains to and from Southport use a rebuilt platform on this site. *Ray DeGroote, Online Transport Archive / J. B. C. McCann*

13

Coverage of the former Lancashire & Yorkshire Railway lines begins at Liverpool Exchange Station. Two miles north, at Walton, the L&Y's line from Bury met tracks from Preston owned by its rival, the East Lancashire Railway. They shared the final section of route into Liverpool to a temporary terminus, built in 1848 at Great Howard Street. Two years later an extension to the existing approach viaduct took the rails on to a shared permanent station, called Exchange by the L & Y, which went on to absorb the ELR in 1859. The Company had already acquired the Liverpool, Crosby And Southport Railway in 1855. As traffic grew the station and its approaches proved to be inadequate, so between 1886 and 1888 the L & Y quadrupled the route from Walton and completely replaced the station. Long distance services took trains as far as Yorkshire, North East England and Scotland. Locally, the growth led to the electrification programme and a more frequent level of service, particularly to Southport, but also to Ormskirk and to Aintree via Marsh Lane. This picture, taken from Platform 7 in the summer of 1974, shows part of the extensive train shed, made up of four gabled roofs supported at either side by solid brick walls. Several 1939 stock EMUs, known by this time as Class 502, were stabled or in service. *M. Eavis, Online Transport Archive*

The Exchange Station of 1888 was a 10 platform terminus, numbers 6 – 10 being electrified. Its popularity waned considerably after World War 2, a location on the edge of the city centre in the business quarter making the railway unattractive to shoppers when compared to the buses of Ribble Motor Services. Exchange became relatively quiet outside the peak hours, a situation made worse by the gradual withdrawal or transfer to Lime Street Station of the long distance services. Platforms 1 – 3 were closed in 1970 and the area used for car parking. When work commenced in 1973 on building the Link that would ultimately see Exchange closed and replaced by an underground station at Moorfields, platforms 8 – 10 were taken out of use and their site used for construction and access. Of the remaining platforms, only numbers 6 and 7 were electrified, so 4 and 5 had conductor rails laid to accommodate the displaced EMUs alongside DMUs used on the one remaining diesel service to Wigan Wallgate and Bolton. This view in May 1975 shows the four platforms and storage siding fully occupied by Class 502s and a Cravens DMU. Note the height difference between the two types of stock. Following the closure of Exchange in May 1977, the cavernous train shed was demolished, part of the site being landscaped whilst the rest is now a car park. *Martin Jenkins, Online Transport Archive*

15

This elevated 1962 panorama shows that the approach to Exchange Station was carried on a mixture of steel and masonry viaducts, underneath a section of which was an L&NWR branch from Edge Hill to the docks. In the centre is the BR built Exchange No. 1 signalbox, the concrete building below it being an LMS era substation for the traction supply. To the left of the signalbox, the brick building with arched openings on the ground floor housed wagon hoists for transferring goods vehicles between two levels, the lower one being the Great Howard Street Goods Yard, constructed on the site of the 1848 temporary terminus. At the very top of the picture Liverpool Exchange Junction can be made out, where the 1850 extension branched off from the original line. Three formations of 1939 stock were seen arriving or departing, whilst a Yorkshire Engine built diesel-hydraulic shunter was stabled in the yard. The warehouses to the right of the road next to the railway viaduct were built to serve the Leeds and Liverpool Canal, which exited the city through the Tate & Lyle sugar refinery seen at the top right. The goods yard shut in 1963, whilst the refinery, many of the warehouses and nearly all the railway infrastructure in this view were later swept away, the concrete ramp into the goods yard marking the alignment of the incline into the 1970s Link line. *A. S. Clayton, Online Transport Archive*

The LC&SR branched off at Sandhills Junction. Trains to Southport negotiate a sharp left hand curve and pull in to Bank Hall Station, which at one time had lengthy canopies over two island platforms, serving four electrified tracks. On 25 April 1971, Driving Trailer M29887M was at the rear of a Southport bound working wearing the Rail Blue livery launched nationally in 1965 and first applied to the 1939 stock three years later. The canopies had gone, together with the platform buildings on the one island still in use, leaving a basic waiting shelter for passengers. Remaining for use by local permanent way staff were the buildings on the other island, serving what were known to railwaymen as the West Lines. The quadruple track continued for some miles but by this date this section of the West Lines was usually only traversed by coal and ballast traffic. Until 1951 they had been used for the service between Exchange and Aintree via Marsh Lane. After that, EMU use was normally limited to peak hour expresses and extras towards Southport. The electrified sidings on the left had been out of use since 1968, largely as a consequence of cutbacks in service frequency. *A. F. Gahan*

Just over 2 miles from Exchange, Bootle Junction is where the L&NWR's route from Edge Hill and Olive Mount to Alexandra Dock, known as the Bootle Branch, meets the Liverpool-Southport line. The L&NWR tracks are on the right of the picture, rising steeply as they emerge from a tightly curved tunnel. Immediately after the junction they fall away before curving to the left, under the L&Y route, to head for the docks. 507 010 passed on a 6-car empty stock working on 15 January 1986, these units being delivered from 1978. By this date part of the West Lines had been dismantled, although the Class 47 waiting to gain the L&NW route provided a reminder that some freight was still carried on these lines, being a working from the Metal Box Company premises at Aintree. The bricked-up opening under the green painted bridge in the background had accommodated the Bankfield Goods Branch, which formerly passed behind the signalbox, descending steeply before curving away towards the docks. The L&NWR had once had their own signalbox at Bootle Junction, but in LMS days it was abolished and total control was passed to the former L&Y box on the left. *Jonathan Cadwallader*

On 9 February 1984, a 507 pulled out of Bootle Oriel Road, bound for Liverpool, whilst on the West Lines, a pair of diesels, 25 199 and 25 231, slowed for a stop at Bootle Junction. The wagons contained track panels made at the since closed Civil Engineer's Yard at Fazakerley, the train having travelled via the North Mersey Branch and Marsh Lane Junction. The L&NWR Bootle Branch, mentioned earlier, passes under the photographer's vantage point in a tunnel, the site of Bootle Balliol Road Station being adjacent to the tunnel mouth. Oriel Road, at one time adorned with canopies, gave an impression of neglect and decay, dispelled in 2008 when the station was substantially rebuilt as part of a programme of upgrades led by Merseytravel, the trading name of the local Passenger Transport Executive.
Rob Marsh

19

Waterloo is so called after a new hotel, the Royal Waterloo, was named to commemorate the 1815 battle. Many fine houses were built here with views over the Irish Sea and North Wales and it became the busiest intermediate call on the line, a position it retains to this day. From Waterloo to the outskirts of Southport the railway is never far from the sand dunes and plays its part in carrying visitors to and from the coastal parks and paths. Sadly, the platform buildings and canopy were demolished in 1975 despite local protests at the loss of the Victorian structures. A handful of passengers were waiting to board on 2 July 1969 as M28344M drew to a halt. Today the railway is so popular that 30-40 would be a typical number of passengers joining an off-peak service at Waterloo. *A. F. Gahan*

Opposition from landowners led to the planned route of the railway through Crosby to be altered, hence the station was named Blundellsands and Crosby, being the best part of a mile from what is still known as Crosby village. This was a bizarre situation as one of the objectors became the railway company's own chairman! The railway was the catalyst that led to the development of Blundellsands as an upmarket residential area, but the position of the line in relation to the centre of Crosby remains an inconvenience to this day. An afternoon working to Southport in the autumn of 1969 saw a class 502 arriving at the platform whilst several ladies and short-trousered schoolboys awaited a Liverpool train. In the Multiple-Unit Green livery introduced in 1956, the set had gained a yellow warning panel below the cab windows as a prelude to the more extensive application of yellow applied to stock repainted from 1968. The station had lost its goods facilities in 1966, but a water tank remained at the end of the down yard, now a car park for rail users. Not long after this photograph was taken, the main station buildings and canopies were demolished, a new booking office being located next to the Liverpool bound platform.

J. G. Parkinson, Online Transport Archive

Hall Road lies at the edge of the continuously built up area. It owes its origin to timber merchant Joseph Gardner, who lived in an isolated house nearby and requested that the L&Y build a new station for his use. The company replied that they would consider the matter should a further five houses ever be constructed close by, whereupon the enterprising Mr. Gardner had them built! In this view on 28 April 1976, an EMU can be seen in the distance occupying a siding once used to reverse terminating trains, by then used for general stock storage. On the opposite side of the line to the bracket signal is one of the LMS concrete substation buildings. On this side of it the Electrical Control Room for the Southport and Ormskirk lines can be made out, now replaced by premises at Sandhills. The 5-car class 502 formation has just completed the 16.53 all stations working from Exchange. It will reverse from this platform and return to Liverpool as empty stock. The large numbers of alighted passengers were waiting to catch the following semi-fast service, which would not have stopped at their stations of origin. In 1939 the large 2-road shed on the left was erected to act as the main depot for routine examinations and light repairs to the new EMUs then being built by the LMS. Disused in recent years, it was demolished in April 2009. *Jonathan Cadwallader*

In April 1989, north of Hightown, a pair of class 507 units approaches the site of Altcar Rifle Range Station. Closing in 1921, it served a military training facility that survives to this day. Part of the platform can be seen opposite the distant signal. 33 x 3-car Class 507 units were built in 1978-80 at York. Their plastic laminate interior lining, fluorescent lighting and thin seat cushions contrasted sharply with the varnished wood, tungsten bulbs and deep sprung, dusty seating of the 502s. Consisting of 2 driving motor cars and an intermediate trailer, each set has 8 x GEC 110hp motors, air suspension, interconnecting carriage doors and a top speed of 75mph. Built for use on the Northern Line, i.e. Southport, Ormskirk and Kirkby to Liverpool Central and south, they can these days also be seen on Wirral services. In the distance was the L&Y power station of 1904. Electricity was generated using steam supplied from 16 Lancashire Boilers, water being drawn from the adjacent River Alt. Coal was brought in to sidings on the site, whilst the ash produced left the building by narrow gauge tramway. In 1947 the generating equipment was worn out and the LMS closed the power station. The building was converted for industrial use but at the time of writing is derelict. *Jonathan Cadwallader*

Just south of Formby Station lies Eccles Crossing. The L&Y signalbox, built in 1912, replaced an earlier structure on the same site. Closure came in March 1994 as a result of the opening of Sandhills Integrated Electronic Control Centre. The line was known for its large number of manual signalboxes, nearly all being adjacent to level crossings. All except Birkdale were demolished after the IECC took over. On 8 May 1965 a rake of 1939 stock headed by M28317M accelerated away from the stop at Formby. These units were built at the LMS Derby Works, deliveries continuing until 1941. Superficially similar to the 1938 Wirral stock, with three front windows in the driving cars and electro-pneumatic sliding doors, they were considerably more powerful, being designed to run at up to 70 mph. Unlike the Wirral sets they were of integral construction, the floor, sides and roof being welded together to provide a strong tubular structure. There were 59 Driving Motor Brake Third cars, 34 Driving Trailer Composites, 50 Trailer Thirds and 9 Trailer Composites. From this total of 152 vehicles, 34 x 3-car units comprising Motor-Trailer-Driving Trailer Composite and 25 x 2-car units formed of Motor-Trailer were derived. The 2-car sets were coupled to a 3-car for service, having a driving position at only one end. Some changes were made over the years, including the conversion of the 9 Trailer Composites to Trailer or Driving Trailer configuration. *B. D. Pyne*

Baggage Cars ran on the line from 1904. They carried parcels, fish, mushrooms, newspapers, asparagus, Royal Mail and internal railway documents, running in between the passenger services. They also transported stores supplies between Meols Cop Car Works in Southport and the depot at Hall Road and to substations. Sitting at the up platform in Formby Station on 8 May 1965 is Baggage Car M68000M. As a BR designed and built unit (rather than LMS,) the M suffix should not have been applied. It started life in 1955, built at Eastleigh as E68000, the only one of its kind, constructed to run on the 600 volt DC, third-rail system on Tyneside. It saw service on Merseyside following the de-electrification of the North East network, but was withdrawn later in 1965 when the parcels service was finished, being scrapped at Meols Cop Car Works in 1967. Note the legend "FISH TRAFFIC THIS END" marked on the side of the car, presumably indicating the presence of an insulated container or the position of drain holes. It is to be hoped that the eventual recipient of the rather battered box lying on the platform did not take delivery of a 487 piece tea service! *B. D. Pyne*

Formby is served by two stations, the other being Freshfield on the north side of the town, adjacent to one of several golf links that are neighbours to the railway between Hall Road and Hillside. This area is well known for the production of high quality asparagus, grown amongst the sand dunes a short distance from the station, but is now more famous for the colony of red squirrels which live in the adjoining pine woods. On 27 January 1979, M28356M pulls out of the station, over the level crossing and heads for Formby with the 14.30 from Southport, the home signal cleared but the distant at caution. English Electric supplied control gear and the four 230hp traction motors for these motor cars, which could easily be distinguished from the Driving Trailers by their roof mounted air intakes. For many years in the BR era the standard timing for trains calling at all 16 stations on the 18 ½ miles between Exchange and Southport was 38 minutes, but there have been countless variations of calling patterns for semi-fast and express trains running to faster schedules. Snowfall as heavy as shown is rare in these parts, but over the years various methods have been employed to prevent ice forming on the conductor rails, from the expedient of running trains all night to spraying a variety of fluids on to the contact surface. *Jonathan Cadwallader*

Serving what is perhaps the most affluent part of Southport, Birkdale Station has retained some of its original ambience. Whilst platform canopies were demolished elsewhere, some of the shelter here has been retained and has recently been refurbished. Out of shot, the large signalbox on the other side of the level crossing has also survived, though out of use. In this early 1979 view, M28349M propels an afternoon Southport bound train out of the station and over the first of the four level crossings that are a feature of the last mile of the line. By this time it was the norm to have a motor car at the city end of 502 formations in order to maximise the speed in the charge out of the northbound platform at Moorfields, before hitting the formidable 1 in 30 gradient to regain the open air. A challenge that proved more difficult to manage was the fact that the stock was almost 40 years old and showing signs of metal fatigue. Without separate underframes, bodywork was often sagging to the point where doors were sticking on a regular basis. Staff carried out a good deal of emergency welding in order to patch the cars together and keep them in traffic until the last sets were withdrawn from normal service in September 1980.

J. G. Parkinson, Online Transport Archive

27

The last of the level crossings on the approach to Southport was at Portland Street. This was the site of the original terminus of the LC &S line and the stationmaster's house of that era survives, being the building on the left of this June 1969 view. Appropriately, this Grade II listed building has a continued railway related role, being the clubrooms of the Southport Model Railway Society. Having cleared the sharp right hand curve that Liverpool trains faced upon departing Southport, Driving Trailer Composite M29880M passed the L & Y signalbox of 1920. This was closed in 1990 once the crossing gates were replaced by automatic barriers. *Cedric Greenwood*

A 1955 view of part of the station throat at Southport. In the background 1939 stock sat on the chord connecting the lines from Liverpool and Wigan, completing a triangle. Platforms 1-3 were electrified for use by Liverpool services. Crossing to Platform 1, slightly obscured by a sign but included for its rarity, was one of two Baggage Cars, M28496M and M28497M, rebuilt at Derby in 1952 from a 1927 2-car compartment set. The traction equipment was divided so that each vehicle had 2 x Metropolitan Vickers 265hp motors. To the right of the car is the Southport substation which still supplies traction current to the line today. The station signalbox on the left of the picture dated from 1917. It housed an early example of a Westinghouse electro-pneumatic frame which passed to the National Railway Museum when the box closed in March 1984. *Ray DeGroote, Online Transport Archive*

During the 19th century, Southport developed into a fashionable seaside resort with an elegant shopping centre. When this view was taken in 1955 there were 10 platforms in the main station with a further 2 for excursion traffic in nearby London Street. The L&Y station was known as Southport Chapel Street to distinguish it from the terminus of the CLC route on Lord Street, half a mile away. The station buildings of 1901 were demolished in 1970 to make way for a shopping development of considerably less architectural worth, but which earned valuable revenue for BR. The platforms and ticket office were then made to hide behind the wall of concrete panels and glass of the shop fronts, like some family member of whom the others were deeply embarrassed. Fortunately the train shed roof over the remaining 6 platforms was kept and has recently been extensively refurbished by Network Rail. In conjunction with Merseytravel, a new booking office/shop, toilets and lighting have also been provided so that the town may have some pride in its station once more. On a sunny May afternoon a 6-car train headed by M28345M set out from Platform 2 wearing lined Malachite Green livery with red buffer beam, the then BR standard colours for EMUs, adopted from the Southern Railway. *Ray DeGroote, Online Transport Archive*

The L & Y route to Preston was energised as far as Crossens on the northern edge of Southport. Over the years the frequency of the electric service varied, but in 1963 there were two or three departures per hour, interspersed with the through trains to and from Preston. Crossens trains usually left from Platform 9 and passed the excursion platforms, carriage sidings, the goods yard and locomotive depot, before reaching St Lukes Junction, three quarters of a mile out. They then swung left to pull in at one of the two island platforms that made up St. Lukes Station, the other being located on the direct Wigan line which closed on 12 June 1965. During the final week of the service, now preserved M29896M was at the rear of a Crossens-bound train in the later green livery that had displaced the malachite shade in 1956. A member of staff escorts the sole passenger, amply coated for the time of year. The Southport-Preston line closed to passengers on Sunday 6 September 1964, the last EMU running the previous night as the electric service had not operated on Sundays for several years. This platform remained open for calls by trains to and from Wigan and beyond, via Meols Cop, until 8 September 1968. *A. S. Clayton, Online Transport Archive*

Close to St. Lukes was the site of the former Hawkshead Street Junction, where the lines to Preston and Wigan via Meols Cop diverged. A chord linked the two lines to form a triangle, in the midst of which were the Meols Cop Car Works, constructed in 1913 for the maintenance of the electric train fleet. In this 1966 view the junction pointwork has been removed and the running lines to and from Preston on the extreme left of the picture have been adapted to form two additional sidings, an armless signal post remaining. The two rakes of non-502 stock were former L&NWR units, built in 1914 for use in the London area, withdrawn after seeing service between Lancaster, Morecambe and Heysham from August 1953 to January 1966.

This line, which had used overhead electrification since 1908, was converted to an experimental AC system. Three surplus 3-car EMUs were rebuilt at Wolverton for their new role with a fourth unit joining them in 1956. Valuable experience was gained in the technology of rectifying and transforming an AC supply to feed DC traction motors in advance of the electrification of other routes, including that from Liverpool Lime Street. These sets were not regular sights at Meols Cop Works but at least one unit visited for a traction motor change, being steam hauled to and from Southport. *J. G. Parkinson, Online Transport Archive*

Meols Cop Car Works concentrated on electrical and mechanical repairs and maintenance, bodywork being dealt with at Horwich Works. Before being towed to Horwich, motor cars had their bogies exchanged for lightweight accommodation examples whilst the regular units were renovated at Meols Cop. In the first view, taken in 1970, a 502 was under repair whilst a quantity of wheelsets awaited attention. The motor bogies were early examples of fabricated rather than cast design and staff were kept busy welding cracks in the frames. Other work carried out here included traction motor, compressor, motor-generator and battery unit overhauls. Control components for traction, braking and doors were serviced, calibrated and tested.

In the second picture Driving Trailer M29864M was receiving attention on 4 September 1969. Between the unit and a stack of bogie frames was an 18 inch gauge railway, used to move components. Unlike the well known 18 inch system at Horwich Works no locomotives were provided, human power being the order of the day. One of the wagons has been preserved by the West Lancashire Light Railway at Hesketh Bank. When Meols Cop Works closed in 1970, its workload was transferred to Birkenhead North. Sets were towed there from Hall Road via Helsby and Dee Marsh Junction, before bodies and motor bogies were separated and the units moved on to Horwich. Since 1983 minor bodywork repairs to Class 507 and 508 units have been handled at Birkenhead North, accident damage being dealt with at Crewe, Doncaster and Wolverton.
J. G. Parkinson, Online Transport Archive / Cedric Greenwood

Returning to the journey to Crossens, from Hawkshead Street Junction a few electric trains bore left for the direct route, achieved in 8 minutes, but most took the right hand fork, in order to call at Meols Cop Station. Shortly after passing Meols Cop Junction, which formed the easternmost point of the triangle, they arrived at the island platform, at which only the Wigan bound track was equipped with a third rail. Electric trains to and from Crossens reversed here. In this September 1964 view, the driver is walking the length of the train, M29865M now being at the rear. The station remains open today as a stop for Southport-Wigan-Manchester diesel units. *Martin Jenkins, Online Transport Archive*

At the northernmost point of the Meols Cop triangle was Roe Lane Junction, just beyond which was Hesketh Park Station, named after nearby Victorian public gardens, the town's largest formal park. In this early 1960s view of a Southport bound service, M29882M was about to welcome a besuited gent to its First Class interior whilst the two ladies further down the platform select the cheaper option. Many of the locals found the town centre near enough to access on foot or used the frequent Corporation bus services, so Hesketh Park was never a source of much passenger traffic outside the peak hours. After the closure of the Southport –Preston line to passengers, Hesketh Park remained open for goods traffic until 1967, access being maintained from Meols Cop.
J. G. Parkinson, Online Transport Archive

3½ miles from Southport Chapel Street, electric trains ended their 13 minute journey on the edge of the town at Crossens, whilst steam hauled services continued to Preston. Trains terminating at Crossens pulled out of the station to the north in order to cross over to the Southport- bound line, or to be recessed in a siding. This manoeuvre was performed with the driver in the rear cab whilst the guard manned the brake in the leading car. A 502 was engaged in this move whilst two local mothers eschewed the delights of the distant cricket match and marshalled their luxurious perambulators prior to boarding the train. Note the oil lamp mounted on the bracket under the cab windows. There were no built-in tail lights at the rear of the 1939 stock until modifications in about 1970. Prior to that date four white marker lights were permanently illuminated in leading cabs, the light concealed behind moveable metal shutters as required. They were wired in series and fed from the 630 volt traction supply, as were the train's interior lights. In practice the two low level lights were not used by staff. The modification work saw the left one converted to a red tail lamp, fed from the unit's 52 volt battery. After this, the practice of displaying an oil headlamp was also discontinued, as the crews were issued with Bardic battery lamps that could be used to display a white light should the traction supply fail. *Martin Jenkins, Online Transport Archive*

Returning to Meols Cop Works, stabled in a siding in August 1962 was Driving Motor M28302M at the head of one of 11 units of compartment stock, built for the LMS as 3-car sets in 1927 to augment the original L & Y fleet. There was also an additional Driving Trailer supplied. Built by the Metropolitan Railway Carriage and Wagon Company in Birmingham, the motor cars were equipped with 4 x 265hp Metropolitan Vickers traction motors. Trailer cars came from Clayton Wagons Ltd of Lincoln, whilst the driving trailers were supplied by the Midland Railway Carriage & Wagon Company of Birmingham. The sets became known to local railwaymen as "Lindberghs", after the American aviator Charles Lindbergh, whose solo Trans-Atlantic flight took place in 1927. Their usual rosters saw them allocated to Liverpool-Ormskirk and Liverpool-Aintree via Marsh Lane duties. The demise of the latter route and a reduction in service requirements saw their withdrawal by 1963 without replacement. *John Rosser*

Moving 7 miles south east of Southport to the busy market town of Ormskirk, M28302M was seen again, captured in early 1962 in a 5-car rake of 1927 stock, not long before final withdrawal. 5 intermediate trailer cars had been moved to the Manchester, South Junction and Altrincham line in 1940, several Lindbergh units becoming 2-car sets. Both main line tracks at Ormskirk were equipped with the third rail, but electric services were usually run from the bay platform, as seen in this view looking towards Liverpool. This left the through platforms free for trains on the Liverpool-Preston main line, though the bay could only hold 5-car trains. In 1962 all stations electric services took 28 minutes to cover the 12 ¼ miles to Exchange. To the north of the station were goods facilities and carriage sidings, some of which were electrified. Ormskirk was once the terminus of other services, to Rainford Junction and St. Helens and to Southport via Burscough. At the top of Station Approach, overlooked by Emmanuel Methodist Church, a dog eyes suspiciously a Bond Minicar, made just up the road in Preston. *J. G. Parkinson, Online Transport Archive*

Through trains from Liverpool to Preston via Ormskirk were withdrawn in 1970. At present, electric trains terminate at buffer stops halfway along the former through line platform for Liverpool. A few yards further north another set of buffer stops marks the end of the line from Preston, served by a DMU a dozen times a day. Shortly before this division took place, a view looking north on 13 May 1970 found M28358M just arrived from Liverpool, having crossed to the southbound platform on its approach ready for the run back to Exchange. This is the only platform left in use today. The Derby DMU was probably working a Liverpool Exchange to Preston or Blackpool turn which would have run fast through most of the stations before Ormskirk. The building on the left still exists today, shorn of its canopy, though not in railway use, whilst that on the right was extensively renovated in 2009. When the route was first split at Ormskirk a loop line was left in, bypassing the buffer stops. Rarely used, it was dismantled a few years later. Recently, fresh studies have taken place to determine the viability of extending the third rail at least as far as Burscough Junction. *J. M. Ryan*

Right: Heading south towards Liverpool and in contrast to the topography of the Southport line, there is a hill to be climbed through a rock cutting, to a summit near to Aughton Park Station. This was originally a simple halt, served by steam railmotors from 1907 until the growth of housing in the vicinity and electrification to Ormskirk in 1913 prompted construction of full sized platforms. On 8 March 1992, 507 030 departed downhill for Liverpool. This route was to see the very last scheduled BR train to use steam traction, being the 21.25 Preston – Liverpool Exchange on the evening of 3 August 1968. The driver of Stanier Class 5 No. 45318 took advantage of the favourable gradient from Aughton Park to urge his charge up to 78mph by the time the train passed Maghull. *David Unwin*

Below: From Town Green and Aughton to Maghull is almost 3 miles of straight track, which allowed drivers to exploit the speed capabilities of the 1939 stock. From 1973 several sets had their intermediate trailer cars stored due to the reduced platform capacity at Exchange and ran as 2-car sets on off-peak Ormskirk services. These sets had an impressive power to weight ratio and stories of speeds of over 80 mph between stops were common. The side to side roll that was a characteristic of the fleet became quite exciting at the higher speeds! However, for the opening of the Link in Liverpool in 1977 the trailers were restored to the sets. Maghull Station retained many of its L & Y features when M28330M headed a southbound service in March 1979. *R. W. Thomson, Online Transport Archive*

Right: Aintree is best known as the home of the Grand National steeplechase, but it was once a major railway centre with two main stations, a substantial quantity of sidings and a large locomotive depot to serve freight from the docks and local industry. From 1912 to 1914 the L & Y had experimented with an electric locomotive, powered from the third rail on running lines and overhead wires whilst in sidings, to haul trains between the North Mersey Goods Yard and Aintree Sorting Sidings. On 29 March 1980, Grand National Day, crowds disgorge from 507s 021 and 004 onto Platform 2, making their way to the adjacent racecourse. On such occasions many extra electric services were run to Aintree, a practice which continues to this day, but to a totally rebuilt station. The trackless Platform 3 had been used by earlier electric services along the North Mersey Branch, by trains from Exchange via Marsh Lane until 1951 and through workings from the Liverpool Overhead Railway for Grand National meetings until 1956. In later years it received excursion trains from many parts of the country. Today the few remaining long distance specials run to Liverpool Lime Street for connections by road coach to the course. This station was known as Aintree Sefton Arms in BR days to distinguish it from the nearby Aintree Central on the former CLC route to Southport. *Jonathan Cadwallader*

Right: A five-car rake of 1939 stock passes Aintree Station Junction, bound for Liverpool in this 1955 view looking south from the Park Lane overbridge, showing the complete provision of third rail. In the distance Aintree East signalbox can be seen on an embankment carrying the North Mersey Branch from Fazakerley Junction on the L&Y's Wigan–Liverpool line. The curve in the picture leads to Sefton Arms Junction where it joined the Branch, carrying on to the docks and Marsh Lane Junction on the Liverpool–Southport line. Lines at Aintree were electrified in 1906, but by this time the third rail on the curve sparked into life on just one day a year between 1951 and 1956 for the annual visit of the LOR stock which, being designed to work from a 500V supply, was required to operate in series only mode when on the BR track. However, there were still regular freight trains over the route. On the extreme right of the picture the line crossed the CLC route, whose Aintree Central station lay in a shallow cutting. Fazakerley Junction to Sefton Arms Junction is now closed and lifted. The remaining part of the Branch itself survives as part of a single track route between Aintree and Bootle Junction, closed to normal traffic but available for engineers' trains as required. Merseytravel has long term aspirations to re-open the line for electric passenger services. *Ray DeGroote, Online Transport Archive*

Heading north, No 507 028 would have been slowing for the stop at Aintree as it passed over the former CLC route to Southport. This was a hopelessly uneconomic line which passed through a largely rural landscape once north of Aintree. It was far too indirect to offer realistic competition to the L&Y routes from Liverpool and Manchester and shut in stages from the Southport end, starting in 1952. Several miles of the alignment now form part of the Southport Coast Road. The regular service south from Aintree Central, which had passed under this bridge, succumbed in 1960 with race meeting specials continuing for a further three years. Services had never been frequent but local trains survived from Gateacre to Liverpool Central until 1972, by which time plans were being laid for the electrification and rebirth of the Liverpool end of the route. *Ted Baxendale*

The station at Walton lies immediately north of the point where the L & Y routes to Preston and Wigan separated. It was known as Walton Junction until 1970, something of a misnomer as the actual junction was at Kirkdale, almost a mile to the south, from which point the four tracks continued to Sandhills. At Walton Junction several railwaymen's cottages had been built adjoining the platform. Being located in the "V" where the routes separated, the residents had the pleasure of a railway at both front and back doors! On 7 August 1969, Driving Trailer Composite M29868M heads a train for Liverpool. A former gas lamp and London Midland Region running in board adorn the platform. *A. F. Gahan*

Now a brief look at developments on the line from Walton Junction to Kirkby, electrified in 1977 and formerly part of the L & Y main line from Liverpool to Manchester. When the Link opened in May of that year, new rolling stock had been ordered to replace the ailing 502 fleet but was not yet delivered. In October 1977, prior to the arrival of the new Class 507s, 2 x 3-car Class 313 units were borrowed from Hornsey Depot in London for testing. Identical in many respects to the 507, these units were also equipped to operate from 25kV AC overhead wires. On what was now called Merseyrail the 313s were used for clearance and performance testing.

One of the main concerns was their ability to cope with the considerable voltage drop on the Ormskirk line caused by the distance between substations. Test equipment included emergency batteries and a set of weights to simulate a load of passengers. 313 013 was seen here at Fazakerley Signal Works Crossing leading 313 063 on the newly electrified section of line, which is single track from Kirkby to this point. It is passing the closed premises of the Railway Signal Company Limited, whose products were exported to all parts of the world. *Ted Baxendale*

Kirkby developed from a farming community to housing an industrial estate, complete with its own railway, together with thousands of people relocated from Liverpool by the slum clearance programme of the 1950s and 1960s. The town became famous for being the inspiration for the BBC police series "Z Cars". The railway was on the edge of the new developments, but electrification and co-ordination of trains with local bus services was seen as the way forward, so the third rail arrived from Walton shortly after the opening of the Link in 1977. The 502 fleet was already fully utilised so 4 x Class 503 units were allocated from Wirral to assist. Due to their relative lack of speed and power they were kept on the route from Kirkby via Liverpool Central to Garston, apart from the odd early morning trip to Ormskirk. Units were rotated from the 503 fleet as they were pushed to their limits to keep to the 502 timings. They carried destination boards in the cab windows as their blinds did not cater for Northern Line destinations. Electrification to Kirkby resolved the issue of what to do with the one remaining diesel service from Liverpool Exchange, that to Bolton. Running the DMUs into the new tunnels was impossible anyway so, following a short period when trains from Bolton terminated at Sandhills, a similar track configuration to that at Ormskirk was introduced at Kirkby. In this January 1978 view, M29145M waits time at the rebuilt station, whilst beyond the back to back buffer stops and the road bridge, a Derby 2-car DMU has arrived from Bolton. *J. G. Parkinson, Online Transport Archive*

43

Left and above: Returning through Walton Junction to resume our journey back to Liverpool, here are two views at Kirkdale, looking north east from the Stanley Road overbridge. They provide a wonderful contrast and show the effects of rationalisation and the end of steam. In the first picture, taken in 1960, the viewer can almost taste the grime as M28348M accelerated past the coal dust covered Sandhills No. 2 signalbox with a morning train from Ormskirk, having just called at Kirkdale Station, the platforms obscured by the bracket signal. To the left was Bank Hall Motive Power Depot, with a 3F "Jinty" 0-6-0T on shed. Bank Hall supplied locomotives for many of the steam-powered services from Exchange and had several Stanier Class 5s and more impressively, three "Jubilee" 4-6-0s for express workings. A fascinating variety of tank engines were also allocated, including some with short wheelbases for shunting on sharply curved dock lines. Beyond the shed building an Ivatt 2-6-2T was busy in the Kirkdale West Carriage Sidings where stock for those trains was serviced. To the right of the EMU were the fast lines used by the L & Y's crack expresses to Manchester Victoria and beyond, which passed behind the platforms at Kirkdale and entered the first of two tunnels on their way to Walton Junction. Further carriage sidings were adjacent before the land sloped away into a cutting, in which lay the CLC's Huskisson Branch, which ran from a junction on its line to Aintree to a large goods depot alongside the L & Y line at Sandhills. To add to the interest, the L&NWR Bootle Branch from Edge Hill, mentioned earlier in the book, runs

obliquely in a tunnel underneath the Kirkdale Station platforms. Kirkdale was a very complicated location, at one time having the lines of three different railway companies crossing each other at three different levels, all of which were below the surrounding roads and housing.

The second picture was taken on 15 July 1979, when everything looked cleaner, if a little less interesting! The MPD had closed in 1966 and over the next few years the fast lines, the sidings and many points and signals were taken out of use, much of the land becoming derelict before BR built Kirkdale EMU Depot in 1976-1977. The loss of siding space in and around Exchange Station was a major factor in determining the need for replacement overnight berthing and the depot was constructed to carry out cleaning, graffiti removal, topping up of fluids, seat repairs and other servicing tasks. In 2006 a wheel lathe was installed. Just a year before they were finally taken out of service a Class 502 rake headed by M28351M was prominent, wearing the Rail Blue and Grey livery first applied to the stock in March 1977. Owing to their forthcoming withdrawal, the 502s had been given special dispensation to operate through the single bore tunnels without having emergency doors cut into the front of the cabs and between each car, modifications which had been carried out on the 503 fleet. To obtain this concession though, parts of the new tunnels were enlarged slightly to accommodate a walkway at the side of the bore, to be used if it was necessary to evacuate a train. *Colour-Rail DE1457 / Jonathan Cadwallader*

Crossing Stanley Road and looking towards the city centre, this is a view of Sandhills Junction, where the lines from Preston and Wigan converged with that from Southport. On 26 July 1971, a class 502 has just left Sandhills Station en route to Ormskirk, the station buildings just visible under the three chimneys of Clarence Dock Power Station. On the right, Class 40 number 340, its turbocharger whistling away, shunted 16-ton mineral wagons full of coal for the merchants who worked from Redfern Street Sidings on the right. This train would have been propelled along the West Lines to this point after a journey from Edge Hill and a reversal at Bootle Junction. Beyond the distant rake of wagons, the North Docks Branch curved off to the right to feed coal and stone drops at Bramley-Moore and Wellington Docks. A few years later the coal traffic and the merchants had gone, the North Docks Branch had closed and the stone trains from Penmaenmawr used Redfern Street, the open wagons being unloaded by a mechanical grab. Today all freight activity has ceased at this location and the 502, the semaphore signals, the 16-ton wagons, the class 40, the sidings, the West Lines, Tillotson Cartons, the block of flats, the pylon and the power station have all gone. Trees and bushes line the railway at this point so that the scene is scarcely recognisable. *A. F. Gahan*

On 27 February 1977, just over 2 months before the Link opened, battery locomotive DB975178/9 descended the recently constructed Leeds Street Bank, heading towards the new tunnels hauling a structure gauge wagon and support van. Converted from two London area Class 501 motor cars, it was an unpopular unit with staff, apparently prone to give electric shocks to the unwary! The derelict building was originally the offices for the Great Howard Street Goods Yard and can be identified on the picture shown earlier in the book. At this time the new tracks had not been permanently connected to the route from Sandhills to Exchange, carried on the steel girder bridge to the right of the building, but class 502s were transferred to the tracks once the traction supply was turned on to allow crew training to take place. This bank in particular was a new experience for drivers and for the rolling stock built for speed on the flat lands of South West Lancashire. Under test the 502s were found to overheat climbing the 1 in 30 gradient, so instructions were issued to signalmen that they were not to be halted there unless absolutely necessary. Exchange Station closed on Friday 29 April 1977, the last passenger train to leave being a diesel-hauled special to Lime Street via Wigan. Tracks were severed and slewed near the top of the bank to join the new formation, ready for the 06.05 departure from Liverpool Central on Monday 2 May. A new electric era had begun. *J. M. Ryan*

After descending the bank, trains call at Moorfields, which effectively replaced Exchange and allows interchange with services on the Loop, which carries trains from Wirral at a deeper level. The new stations made extensive use of fibreglass and laminates in brown, cream and white. One of the authors (JAC) was approached by the man on the platform who asked if the train was going to Central. Assured that it was, his attention was drawn to a sign confirming the fact. Clearly not believing his ears or his eyes, he then knocked on the driver's door and made the same enquiry. The driver nodded confirmation, received the two-bell signal from the guard and set off, leaving the doubter on the platform! Trains continue under the city before the tunnels break into the now replaced former Mersey Railway double track bore at Paradise Junction. They thus approach what had been Liverpool Central Low Level and call at the rebuilt island platform. By reversing at Central, units can fork left at Paradise Junction and gain access to the former MR line at James Street. This single track connection is to enable stock to be transferred between what are now known as the Northern and Wirral Lines and is not for passenger use. *Jonathan Cadwallader*

Garston Station was rebuilt to be the southern terminus of the Northern Line. Driving Trailer M29870M is at the rear of a train from Kirkby. Work on the other platform started when funds were found to extend the third rail to Hunts Cross in July 1983, allowing interchange with trains from Lime Street to Warrington Central and the east. Services were amended so that trains from Southport rather than Kirkby ran south from Central. Just east of the station the line passed under the Liverpool-Crewe route at the end of the platforms of Allerton Station. A plan to combine the two stations came to fruition on 11 June 2006 when Liverpool South Parkway was opened, with four platforms on the Crewe and Warrington tracks and two on the Northern Line, the latter replacing Garston Station, since demolished. *R. W. Thomson, Online Transport Archive*

The CLC's Liverpool Central High Level closed on 17 April 1972, the last remaining service being to Gateacre on the erstwhile route to Aintree and Southport. For most of the stations served by these final trains though, closure was to be less than six years long. Following completion of the Link scheme, trains from the north of the city were able to climb a grade from Central to access the former CLC tunnel and route. Services commenced on 3 January 1978, initially between Kirkby and Garston. Whilst some of these workings utilised class 503 units transferred from Birkenhead, the 502s were also in evidence. M28358M pulls in to Cressington on 12 May 1978, leading a Garston bound service. This station is in a conservation area and had kept most of its Victorian glory at a time when the majority of the stations north of the city had lost theirs. It was thoroughly renovated before reopening, the work including the reinstallation of Midland Railway lamp columns, brought in from elsewhere on BR. *David Ventry*

Leaving third-rail territory for a while, a look next at part of the Liverpool-Crewe route, on the London and North Western Railway's main line to the capital. It was electrified using the 25kV AC overhead wire system as part of the BR London Midland Region scheme of the 1960s. Basking in the sun at Allerton Depot, on 20 October 1963, at the head of a line of locomotives was AL1 number E3011, resplendent in its Electric Blue livery, embellished with white painted cab roofs and windows, cast crest and numbers. Ordered as far back as 1955 from the British Thompson Houston division of AEI, as part of the first batch of 25kV locomotives, E3011 was delivered in November 1960. She was assembled at the works of The Birmingham Railway Carriage And Wagon Company, acting as sub-contractor to BTH. Later becoming 81 009, the locomotive was scrapped in 1991. The depot, which also serviced diesel locomotives and multiple units, saw its workload diminish gradually following the withdrawal of the 1950s DMU fleet and is currently mothballed. *Brian Faragher*

Ditton Junction was opened by the L&NWR in 1871, primarily to provide facilities for passengers to change trains as this was not a residential area. BR totally rebuilt the station in 1961 but services to Manchester, Chester and North Wales were soon withdrawn, leaving just an hourly Liverpool – Crewe train. Passenger numbers continued to fall at Ditton (the Junction suffix was dropped in 1973) and the station was closed on 27 May 1994. The buildings have since been demolished. In this view, taken on 9 December 1961, the secondman of E3065, new that month, looked back as he awaited a clear road east of the station. It was one of 40 AL5 electric locomotives built by BR at Doncaster with A.E.I. equipment. Later renumbered 85 010 and briefly to 85 103, it was scrapped in 1992. Note the twin pantographs, common to the AL1-AL5 classes when new. *J. M. Ryan*

Allerton Station was rebuilt by BR in a similar style to that employed at other locations on AC lines in the North West. On 14 April 1971 AM4 electric multiple-unit 014 pulled out of Platform 1 on its way to Crewe. Later known as Class 304, 45 of these EMUs were built at Wolverton, being employed mainly to the north of Rugby. They were notorious for their lively ride; their bogies, designed by Sir Nigel Gresley, seemed ill-suited to speeds of up to 75 mph, giving passengers many exciting and even alarming moments when negotiating junctions or less than perfectly aligned trackwork! The last one was withdrawn in 1996. Allerton Station is no more, being totally rebuilt and enlarged as Liverpool South Parkway, as related earlier. *A. F. Gahan*

BR launched "The Liverpool Pullman" in 1966 using carriages from a fleet of 29 air-conditioned vehicles purpose-built for this and a similar service from Manchester, in a reverse version of the new Rail Blue and Grey scheme. The service normally consisted of four Pullman cars marshalled ahead of Second Class Mark 1 vehicles. On 29 April 1975, locomotive 86 240 was seen from the Penny Lane bridge in Mossley Hill with an up working, on this occasion missing one of the Pullman cars. 100 AL6, or Class 86, were built in 1965-66, construction being divided between Vulcan Foundry and BR's Doncaster Works, using equipment supplied by English Electric and AEI. 86 240 had been new as E3127 and was classified as an 86/2 in 1973. *David Ventry*

Edge Hill is the oldest working railway station in the world, being built in 1836 by the Liverpool and Manchester Railway. It stands immediately east of the tunnels and cutting leading down to Lime Street station. The sandstone buildings and walls of the original station were later given brick-built extensions. Other tunnels either side of Edge Hill station gave access to the docks, Riverside station and a variety of goods yards, including that at Crown Street, site of the original Liverpool and Manchester terminus. In this view, 87 024 *Lord of the Isles* breasted the climb from Lime Street on 2 May 1984, hauling the empty stock of the Royal Train. 36 Class 87s were built using GEC equipment by British Rail Engineering Limited at Crewe between 1973 and 1975 and they were daily visitors to Liverpool. After final withdrawal in 2007, many were exported to Bulgaria but 87 024 met its end in a South Wales scrapyard in 2005. *Rob Marsh*

East of Edge Hill station was the first large marshalling yard in Britain. Built by the L&NWR in 1873, it took advantage of a natural slope to the west to allow gravity shunting. It was colloquially known as "The Gridiron" and was built to eliminate the congestion caused by the level of traffic and conflict of routes. A complementary scheme known as the Circular Railway was designed to give direct access to and from the Crewe route without having to cross the Manchester line on the level. Examination of this breathtaking photograph, looking east from within the premises of Crawford's Biscuits on 24 November 1965, gives an idea of the level of complexity and might tempt the curious to consult an old map! The company's green fireless locomotive was at the head of a rake of vans. Immediately to the right was the pair of lines giving access to the Manchester route. Next was the Circular Railway, with a Stanier 8F hauling a mixed freight from the Crewe line underneath the sorting sidings whilst a Class AL6 in early Rail Blue headed in the opposite direction. At a higher level were freshly ballasted roads that bypassed the yards and then the eastern ends of some of the sidings. The original L&MR route is at a lower level in the haze beyond the yards. The Bootle Branch still exists underneath this view, but Crawford's, all the yards and their access routes have gone. Wavertree Technology Park and station now occupy most of this site. *Brian Faragher*

The approach to Liverpool Lime Street is one of the most memorable of any station in Britain. Opened in 1836, it replaced the original L&MR terminus of 1830 at Crown Street. One can only marvel at the successive engineering feats using very basic equipment that resulted in the route as experienced today. First, a mile long double track tunnel was excavated from Edge Hill, to allow rope hauled trains to descend the 1 in 93, steepening to 1 in 83, gradient. As locomotive designs evolved, they became sufficiently powerful to enable rope haulage to be discontinued in 1870, the tunnel being opened out in many places by 1881 to allow smoke to disperse.

Then, by 1890, the formation was widened to take four tracks with many substantial stone bridges being required to span the cutting. The platform ends are visible in the distance as EMU 310 084 started its climb to Edge Hill on 24 July 1976. Introduced in 1965 as Class AM10, these 50 4-car units were built at Derby to a design derived from that for the BR Mk II loco-hauled coach and were a considerable advance on the earlier AM4. Not common in Liverpool, being more usually employed on workings from London Euston and Birmingham, summer Saturdays in the 1970s saw a regular return journey from Birmingham New Street. *J. M. Ryan*

Arrival at Lime Street is always an enlightening experience as your train emerges from the gloom of the cutting, the stonework partially blackened by generations of steam locomotives. Preparatory work for the installation of the overhead wires was started in 1959, one of the first locations to be equipped following the experimental AC scheme on the Lancaster-Heysham route as described earlier. AL1 E3016 protruded slightly beyond the end of platform 7 at the head of the 10.30 to London Euston on the 14 May 1969, the train crew making ready for departure. To the left of the locomotive was a pair of sidings, accessed through the stone pillar supporting the bridge that carries Copperas Hill over the station and useful for holding locomotives and vans. In 1966 several London trains ran via Birmingham, but as what was known as the "sparks effect" took hold, passenger numbers mushroomed and more frequent, direct services were added. E3016 became 81 014 in later years and was scrapped in 1991. *E. V. Richards*

The official date for the start of electric working between Liverpool and Crewe was 1 January 1962, the month that AL2 number E3053 was new. On the 23 July that year she waited at the end of Platform 5. Hanging out of the cab windows, two footplate staff looked across the station throat, still wearing the traditional greasetop caps of the steam era. In the background, safety valves blowing off, was one of Sir William Stanier's "Princess Coronation" class, commonly known as "Duchesses". Withdrawal of Stanier's earlier "Princess Royal" class Pacifics, residents of Edge Hill shed for many years, had already started. Soon the "Coronations" would follow. E3053 was in a class of only 10, being amongst the second tranche of locomotives ordered for the AC Lines. It came from another part of the AEI empire, Metropolitan Vickers, with construction sub-contracted to Beyer Peacock at Gorton. Unlike the other early AL classes, which were of integral or semi-integral construction , the AL2s had separate underframes, making them the heaviest of the designs, though this quality gave them a better ride than most. Once the AL6 class were all in traffic, the AL2s were largely used on freight and parcels trains. E3053 later became 82 007, but being non-standard at a time when BR had more locomotives than it needed, was scrapped in 1984. *J. M. Ryan*

This page: Exploration of the former Mersey Railway (MR) and LMS electrified Wirral services begins in the depths of the terminal station at Liverpool Central Low Level with two views taken in July 1975, just before it closed for reconstruction to serve the Northern Line. They show the beams supporting the High Level station, the varied bookstalls and kiosks which were set to disappear and the headshunt, later to become part of the new extended tunnel. Having arrived at Central, the driver walked to the rear of the train and reversed it into the headshunt. Once the electro-pneumatic points had switched over and the signal turned to green, he took the train into the Down platform ready for departure. In peak hours, to maintain the 2½ minute headway (5 mins. Rock Ferry and 10 mins. each on New Brighton and West Kirby,) reversals were handled by a "turn-over" crew. In 1921, automatic signals and track circuiting were installed in the tunnel but the two signalboxes at Low Level remained open until automatic reversing was introduced in 1923. These signalboxes were subsequently retained for emergency use only. The third view shows M28385M at James Street on 17 March 1984 when Wirral services terminated here due to re-railing work on the Loop. This original MR terminus was on a gradient of 1:100, the steepest under-river gradient being 1:27. Since the Loop opened, only the westbound platform of the original station remains in regular use. *G. D. Parry / J. M. Ryan / Rob Marsh*

Hamilton Square, the busiest of the former MR stations in Birkenhead, still enjoys a high level of service. Like James Street, it is on a gradient of 1:100, the ascent from the river being 1:30. This view shows the station after it was modernised and re-designed as part of the Loop and Link programme. The indicator shows the original "Liverpool Loop" destination. To increase trains per hour, a burrowing junction opened in May 1977 enabled West Kirby and New Brighton trains to pass under the Rock Ferry line, although shortly afterwards peak hour headways were reduced. Owing to the curvature of the platforms, guards on 6-car trains could not see the green departure signal, therefore in peak hours a staff member known as "Six-Car" watched on the platform for the green signal, at which point he held a white light towards the guard. *W. Watters*

Opened in 1888 and shared with the Wirral Railway, Birkenhead Park was administered by a Joint Committee. Until 1938, passengers changed between the MR and the WR services to New Brighton and West Kirby. When the latter routes were electrified by the LMS, Park was where the changeover took place between the MR fourth rail and the LMS third rail systems. On MR trains this took place automatically in both directions. On LMS stock it only occurred in the Liverpool direction, drivers bound for Birkenhead North having to operate a switch in the cab.

This situation prevailed until 1955 when, for their final months, MR stock operated entirely on the third rail. The disused fourth rail was still in place in July 1956 as a 1903 1st Class motor car headed a Liverpool-bound train into the Up platform. Prior to 1971, Park had two island platforms, one for each direction, as well as a range of sidings. Until 1979, it was a major bus interchange. Today, everything is greatly simplified. *D. Kelso, Colour-Rail DE1886*

This page: The first view, taken on 25 July 1972, depicts a 503 in the cutting between Birkenhead Park and Birkenhead North, flanked on the left by the former Corporation bus garage and on the right by municipal flats, now demolished. For years, this cutting was littered with all manner of debris. M28673M was one of nineteen 3rd class motor cars built in 1938. In the second view, taken on 17 May 1955, a pre-war Birkenhead Massey-bodied Leyland crested Ilchester Road, as a train of original MR stock arrived at Birkenhead North, the leading carriage being one of 17 x 3rd class trailers with control equipment at either end. To its right was the control room installed by the LMS in 1938, power being supplied by Liverpool Corporation at 11kV AC and converted to 650V DC at local substations. The LMS adopted the national standard position for the positive conductor rail at 16in. from and 3in. above the gauge rail as opposed to 22in. and 5in. on the MR. Whilst the MR was converted, their motor cars had double pick-up shoes and modifications for running over the newly-electrified sections, including a "deadman" facility. *G. D. Parry / Ray DeGroote, Online Transport Archive.*

This page: By May 1955, the old MR stock had been dubbed "Grandad's Railway" by some newspapers. Although upgraded in the late 1930s, the carriages compared unfavourably with the "art deco" streamlined LMS stock. The delivery of 24 similar 3-car sets, plus four additional units as replacements for war damaged stock, allowed for withdrawal of the last MR train on 12 June 1957. No.1 was set aside for preservation, but was sadly lost in a fire. In 2010 the former WR station building at North, together with the Stationmaster's house (1878) on the Down platform survive, as does the canopy on the Up island platform, but the cover over the footbridge and the small inspector's cabin have gone. On the Down platform, the illuminated "Next Train" indicator has been replaced. Star of the second scene was M28794, (ex-MR No. 58,) one of 11 original 1st class trailers which had been rebuilt with a welded steel body and flush windows following war damage. *Ray DeGroote, Online Transport Archive (2)*

In 1938, the LMS opened the workshop and depot facility at Birkenhead North. As there is no third rail "juice" supply within the building, trains are powered by means of a cable attached to the shoes and connected to an overhead supply. Traditionally, North operated the West Kirby service whilst Birkenhead Central covered Rock Ferry and New Brighton. However, to ensure network-wide familiarity, roles were reversed on Sundays. Following closure of Meols Cop and Hall Road, North now handles heavy maintenance for the entire electric network. Today, some of the stock for the Wirral line is provided from Kirkdale depot. These movements, together with stock heading to North for maintenance, use Paradise Junction, referred to earlier. *Alan Hodges*

Seacombe Junction box, destroyed by arsonists in 1989, handled traffic to and from Bidston Dock sidings (left background) as well as traffic on the New Brighton and Seacombe lines. Plans to electrify the Seacombe branch were never realised and it closed in 1963, some of the track bed forming part of the approach road to the Kingsway road tunnel. Diverted on 19 September 1971, owing to engineering works, this 6-car unit was working from West Kirby to New Brighton using the curve from Bidston West Junction. This curve, now severed and reduced to siding status at the Bidston end, was used between 1923 and 1939 by through New Brighton-London carriages and from 1960 to 1971 (Sundays until 1976) by DMUs on New Brighton-Chester/Wrexham services. Latterly, there was also a single scheduled one-way EMU working from West Kirby to New Brighton. In 1973, the 43 Wirral EMU sets were classified as 503s. Ready for operating round the Loop, they had end doors fitted for emergency evacuation. *J. M. Ryan*

Whereas the MR carved its way through central Birkenhead, lines serving Wallasey skirted the areas of population. When the New Brighton branch opened in 1888, there were two intermediate stations of which Wallasey (later Wallasey Grove Road) had an impressive approach road and a fine brick-built building which is still extant. Although in an area of low-density housing, it was close to the shore and later, a popular open air swimming pool. The goods and coal yard seen on the right closed in 1965. During winter months, beach huts had been stored in its goods shed. On a cold February morning in 1971, a handful of passengers wait to board a 6-car Liverpool-bound train. The Rail Blue livery with yellow panel beneath the driver's window first appeared on Wirral EMUs in 1967. A series of four-aspect headlamp codes identifying journeys over particular sections was dropped in later years.
A. F. Gahan

This page: Two rare 1954 scenes of MR trains near the site of Warren Station, closed in 1916. Heading the first train was one of the original 13-window 1st Class wooden-bodied motor cars. Built by GF Milnes in 1903, they had air brakes and four 100hp motors. Their clerestory roofs, match-board panels and Baldwin bogies gave them a distinctly American flavour. The later provision of master controllers in the driving trailers allowed for MU operation whilst automatic couplers and buffers speeded up the removal and addition of carriages. Leading the second view was one of two 3rd Class motor cars, part of a group of seven wooden-bodied Craven-built carriages from the mid-1920s. These, and subsequent deliveries, had domed ends, elliptical roofs and wider windows with top lights. After 1936, with the odd exception, the stock was in 3-car sets, although the carriages in the formations were not fixed. One writer recalls the thrill of a ride, particularly at night. "Great blue flashes illuminated the tunnel walls, the interior lights flickered on and off especially at junctions and on tight curves when the creaking carriages jostled and bounced against each other and the long hanging straps slapped rhythmically on the roof."(MJ)
J. B. C. McCann (2)

Initially founded as an upmarket dormitory for Liverpool, New Brighton developed into a lively resort frequented especially by day trippers from the city who came by ferry and after 1888, by rail. Although the Tower (taller than Blackpool) was taken down after World War 1, the resort flourished until changes to holiday and travel patterns led to a decline from the 1950s onwards. In early 1961, a DMU stands on the north side of the island platform, to which the 230ft concrete canopy had been added at the time of electrification. Off-peak and overnight storage sidings existed on both sides. Now preserved, M28690M was one of the nineteen 3rd class motor cars known as 1938 stock, the suffix M indicating a unit built either for the LMS or to one of their designs. Today, an industrial estate occupies the former coal and goods yard closed in 1965, whilst the Winter Gardens theatre on the far left has been demolished. The imposing WR station of 1888 with its high, panelled booking hall survives.
E. J. McWatt, Online Transport Archive

Back again at Birkenhead North on 17 May 1955 with Driving Motor car M28686M about to embark on the 6¼ mile journey to West Kirby. Until the replacement of the ex-MR stock in 1956, the West Kirby line was operated by the 1938 stock Monday-Saturday and by MR sets on Sundays. The 1938 Stock featured all-steel lightweight saloon bodies of fully welded construction, each having two pairs of air-operated sliding doors on either side. The 58-seater motor cars had four 135hp motors. This set was in the malachite green applied by BR to all its MU stock from 1949 until 1956. This livery had replaced the striking maroon of the LMS units and the more sombre red and brown carried by the MR trains. Whilst the oldest MR trains clocked up 53 years service, some of these pre-war LMS sets lasted for 45 years. The former WR Birkenhead North No 1 signalbox was painted in standard BR London Midland Region colours. *Ray DeGroote, Online Transport Archive.*

A remarkable scene looking over Bidston Moss on 31 May 1967 when EMUs operating between Birkenhead North and Bidston still crossed the tracks (now lifted) leading from Birkenhead Docks to the former Great Central goods sidings, seen on the right with a diesel shunter in attendance. Waiting for a West Kirby-bound EMU to clear Bidston West Junction was 92120, a BR Standard 9F on an iron ore train from Bidston Dock (in the background) to the John Summers steelworks at Shotton. The bark from the exhaust on these 2-10-0s storming Storeton bank echoed across the whole area. Having just left Bidston station, the DMU was en route to New Brighton. Today, freight traffic has ended, Bidston Dock is filled in, the GC sidings have been lifted and traffic on the M53 roars above the foreshortened curve to Seacombe Junction, now reduced to a siding. *A. F. Gahan*

Once in semi-rural isolation, Bidston Station (1896) is now almost surrounded by roads. The island platform was improved for the 1938 electrification but, owing to the foundations being constructed on marshland, the light, wooden WR buildings were retained, staff always taking care to check the fire-buckets. Access is by means of a footbridge from which this view was taken in 1967. Painted in the dark green MU livery adopted in 1956 and carrying a partial yellow front to improve visibility, this EMU had just completed the fast ¾ mile run across open country from Leasowe as empty stock, whilst the DMU was taking the sharp curve onto the mid-Wirral line. Since 1978, trains on the mid-Wirral line have terminated at Bidston. Built by the LMS in 1937, Bidston Dee Junction signalbox was closed in 1994 and demolished. Although coal and goods traffic ceased in 1968, the last of the GC sidings, on the left, were not lifted until the early 1980s. *Marcus Eavis, Online Transport Archive.*

Although the single track Hoylake Railway (1866) originally served lightly populated areas of farmland, it gradually encouraged population growth with increasing numbers opting to live on Wirral but work in Liverpool. When the line was doubled, a new station was opened at Leasowe in 1894. This view was taken 100 years later when, following closure of the signalbox, the semaphores were being operated from the temporary box on the left and the gates by the man in the high visibility jacket. Previously, the crossing gates were opened and closed by a signalman using a large wheel in the box. In 2010 queues of traffic still form here each time a train passes through. Heading for Liverpool was 508 103, one of 43 sets of class 508 built by BR at York and transferred from the Southern Region to replace the 503s. It was in the MPTE livery introduced in 1991. *Charles Roberts, Online Transport Archive.*

During spells of fine weather, trains were frequently packed with people heading for the beaches close to the stations at Moreton, Hoylake and West Kirby. Trains serving Moreton Station, which lay some distance from the town centre, were in competition with Birkenhead and Wallasey Corporation buses, both of which offered combined bus and ferry tickets for travellers from Liverpool. On 13 November 1971, one of the 1956 Driving Trailers, M29135M, was en route to West Kirby. At this stage, stock numbers were displayed at the bottom offside. Although the line once handled a degree of freight traffic, most facilities had closed by 1965. However, the Cadbury's biscuit factory (left background) was served by rail from 1953 until 1971. The signalbox on the left controlled movements in and out of the factory, loaded vans leaving via the mid-Wirral line, or until 1962, via West Kirby and Hooton. Latterly, the vans accessed the Birkenhead-Chester line by way of Birkenhead Docks.
A. F. Gahan

Hoylake was transformed by the coming of the railway in 1866 into a prosperous dormitory for Liverpool. In preparation for electrification, new "art deco" buildings of brick and reinforced concrete were provided at Leasowe, Moreton, Meols and Hoylake, the latter being the most substantial with its cantilevered canopy, striking frontage on the Up side, impressive entrance hall, booking office and small retail outlets. Platform facilities included staff rooms, waiting rooms and toilets. The area in the right background once housed the Hoylake Railway facilities as well as access tracks to the town's gas works. The coal yard was closed in 1965. Overnight storage sidings existed on both sides of the main line but by September 1979 only the one on the south side remained. When all three were in use, an early morning staff train was run from Birkenhead North. M28381M was one of 24 Second Class 58-seater Driving Motor Cars built by MCCW in 1956. The full yellow fronts added in the late 1960s hardly added to their overall appearance. *Marcus Eavis, Online Transport Archive*

Between Hoylake and West Kirby the line swings in a south-westerly direction, overlooked on one side by golf links and on the other by Victorian villas. This corner of Wirral was definitely "up market" and for decades, the 1st class seats on 6-car peak hour trains from Hoylake and West Kirby were filled with bowler-hatted businessmen travelling into town. The off-peak 3-car trains were frequented by those going to the city's shops and places of entertainment and in term time by local school children. In this September 1979 view, a Liverpool-bound set approached the level crossing at the west end of Hoylake station, the signals and crossing gates being controlled from the former WR signalbox which was demolished after it closed in 1994. The crossing gates are now automatic. On the left was one of the line's substations. *Marcus Eavis, Online Transport Archive*

Essentially residential with quality shops and excellent views over the River Dee, West Kirby, some 10 miles from Low Level, also attracted day trippers. The present station, surmounted by its clock tower, dates from 1896 and the extended concrete canopy over the island platform from 1937. The new fire station under construction in March 1976 was being built on the site of the first railway station of 1878. Today, the signalbox and semaphore signals have gone and only three sidings remain, one on the west side of the platform and two on the east. In 2010 the station area contains shops and the booking office is located in a new, unprepossessing building dating from the 1980s. Until 1962, there had been a junction in the foreground with tracks curving away to the left. They connected with the separate West Kirby Joint station, one-time terminus of the L&NW/GW branch from Hooton. *Jonathan Cadwallader*

This page: Until 1983, the Class 503s went every four years to Horwich Works for a major overhaul and repaint. No M29284M was at the head of a set ready to depart from Birkenhead North for what would have been its final overhaul when seen on 19 November 1980, having had its footboards removed for clearance purposes. Until 1962 the route was via the West Kirby–Hooton branch, sets later travelling via the mid-Wirral line. In the second scene, outside the Horwich paintshop on 13 October 1963 was one of two hybrid three-car sets. These featured 1938 motor cars and 1956 trailers, the latter, including No M29156M shown here, being built to replace cars destroyed during the war. The non-driving trailer (M29823M) clearly shows the band at cantrail level designating it to be a composite 1st/2nd class car. First class was abolished in the early 1970s. Each view includes one of the 'match wagons' needed for the journey to and from Birkenhead. These had different couplings at either end, a buckeye to match the electric units and a conventional shackle to match with a locomotive or guard's van. *Charles Roberts, Online Transport Archive / Colour-Rail*

Birkenhead Central, ½ mile from Hamilton Square and close to the business, commercial and entertainment districts, was once the headquarters of the MR. On the left were a stationmaster's house, a large booking hall and various offices, including those of the General Manager and Engineer. Strict time-keeping for trains was a priority. In times past, an engineer was sent into the tunnel "at the run" to resolve any delay exceeding five minutes. To the right of the platforms were various sidings and adjacent to these, at the rear of the carriage sheds, the cramped workshop, closed in 1956. Until nationalisation, the MR had a solitary steam locomotive for ballast work. At the bottom left was the last MR signalbox to survive. Once controlling movements within the complex, it eventually fell into disuse and was broken up. Much of the skyline has now disappeared, although the tower of Birkenhead Town Hall can still be seen. *Martin Jenkins, Online Transport Archive*

Just ¼ mile from Central, Green Lane was the MR terminus from 1886 until 1891. The platforms occupy a deep cutting with high, moss-stained, retaining walls and are unusual in that the Down side is sheltered under a brick vaulted ceiling whilst the Up side is open to the elements. The 1891 extension to Rock Ferry tackles the mainly 1:35 incline in the background. The overbridge, which could not be raised or lowered to accommodate wires, was one reason why the MR opposed LMS proposals to convert to the overhead wire system in the 1930s. Now often deserted, Green Lane was once busy with shipyard workers. The Rock Ferry service ran once every five minutes in peak hours with 6-car trains. The former "Alight for Tranmere and Cammell Lairds" sign on the Down platform has been replaced in recent years by a smaller "Alight here for Lairdside". *Jonathan Cadwallader*

This page: The 1891 extension to Rock Ferry gave the MR access to lucrative traffic from the Wirral hinterland. The MR paid the L&NW/GW Joint to use their tracks (which the MR maintained) and for terminal facilities. M28423, formerly MR motor car 30, was unique. After suffering heavy war-damage, its 6½ window welded-steel saloon body with transverse seating was built at Wolverton in 1942. Here, at the start of its 3½ mile trip it passed vintage signals as well as a LN&W signalbox together with its BR replacement opened in 1956. The second view, taken on 6 March 1976, shows the stub terminal at the west side of the station with its two bay platforms and storage siding. Both Driving Trailers were built by BRCW; M29135M, stabled on the siding, dated from 1956 and M29279M from 1938. In 1985, the track layout at Rock Ferry was redesigned for through running onto the electrified extension to Hooton. The station facilities have also been greatly reduced.
J. B. C. McCann / Jonathan Cadwallader

This page: Prior to withdrawal of the last 503s on 29 March 1985, a 3-car set of 1938 stock repainted in LMS maroon took part in several farewell tours. On 30 September 1985 it passed through Spital on a special working during the first day of operation of the 6 mile electrified extension to Hooton. To the right were the remains of the former fast lines. After operating Christmas specials, the 503 then starred in the 1986 MR centenary celebrations. It is now in the care of the Suburban Electric Railway Association near Coventry but is not on public view. In the second picture, taken at Hooton in 1990, passengers transferred from 508 105 onto a 2-car Derby DMU bound for Ellesmere Port and Helsby. Opened in 1840, Hooton became a junction with six through platforms and one bay, but during the 1960s it fell into decline until revitalised by the electrification programme. Today's present integrated network was completed when the third rail was extended firstly to Chester in 1993 and then to Ellesmere Port in 1994.
Jonathan Cadwallader (2)

It seems appropriate to complete this electric journey at Birkenhead Central, one of the area's last surviving historical sites. As late as August 1969, a solitary traction pole (bottom right) offered a reminder of the town's electric trams (1901-1937). This view captures the cramped nature of the complex with its workshops, depot and station all confined at the southern extremity of the tunnel in a cutting flanked on the east side by the gas works and on the west by Argyle Street South with its rows of terraced housing. The 1886 MR locomotive and carriage sheds can be seen adjacent to the gas works wall as well as the electric workshops with the later extension built on the front. The entrance to the works was alongside Central Taxis and to the station under the neglected iron and glass canopy. In the far distance is part of Mollington Street locomotive shed (closed in 1985), where one of the last activities was the scrapping of redundant 503s. In 2010, renovated Birkenhead Central still carries the legend "Mersey Railway - Quickest Route To Liverpool" on the gable end.
G. D. Parry